discovermore

Economics in Your Community

Jobs and Earnings

Sloane Wilden

I0806699

Britannica Educational Publishing

IN ASSOCIATION WITH

THE ROSEN PUBLISHING GROUP

Published in 2024 by The Rosen Publishing Group, Inc.
2544 Clinton Street, Buffalo, NY 14224

Editor: Brianna Propis
Book Design: Michael Flynn

Photo Credits: Cover Monkey Business Images/Shutterstock.com; (series background) Dai Yim/Shutterstock.com; p. 5 top VAKS-Stock Agency/Shutterstock.com; p. 5 bottom hedgehog94/Shutterstock.com; pp. 6, 10 Andrey_Popov/Shutterstock.com; p. 7 Ground Picture/Shutterstock.com; p. 8 Ja Crispy/Shutterstock.com; p. 9 Blue Planet Studio/Shutterstock.com; p. 11 Jacob Lund/Shutterstock.com; p. 12 Anel Alijagic/Shutterstock.com; p. 13 Dragana Gordic/Shutterstock.com; p. 15 (bottom) a katz/Shutterstock.com; p. 15 (top) PeopleImages.com-Yuri A/Shutterstock.com; p. 16 SeventyFour/Shutterstock.com; p. 17 Timmary/Shutterstock.com; p. 19 (bottom) Dusan Petkovic/Shutterstock.com; p. 19 (top) Studio Peace/Shutterstock.com; p. 21 (top) Taya Ovod/Shutterstock.com; p. 21 (bottom) Rawpixel.com/Shutterstock.com; p. 22 Yeongsik Im/Shutterstock.com; p. 23 Drazen Zigic/Shutterstock.com; p. 24 Ground Picture/Shutterstock.com; p. 25 Daenin/Shutterstock.com; p. 26 Kristi Blokhin/Shutterstock.com; p. 27 fizkes/Shutterstock.com; p. 29 (bottom) CSNafzger/Shutterstock.com; p. 29 (top) Elle Aon/Shutterstock.com.

Library of Congress Cataloging-in-Publication Data

Names: Wilden, Sloane, author.
Title: Jobs and earnings / Sloane Wilden.
Description: [Chicago, IL] : Britannica Educational Publishing, [2024] | Series: Discover more: economics in your community | Includes bibliographical references and index.
Identifiers: LCCN 2023030603 | ISBN 9781641900300 (library binding) | ISBN 9781641900294 (paperback) | ISBN 9781641900317 (ebook)
Subjects: LCSH: Vocational guidance--Juvenile literature. | Labor--Juvenile literature. | Wages--Juvenile literature.
Classification: LCC HF5381.2 .W53 2024 | DDC 331.702--dc23/eng/20230801
LC record available at https://lccn.loc.gov/2023030603

Manufactured in the United States of America

Some of the images in this book illustrate individuals who are models. The depictions do not imply actual situations or events.

CPSIA Compliance Information: Batch #CWBRIT24. For further information contact Rosen Publishing at 1-800-237-9932.

Contents

Welcome to the Working Week

When you order food or choose an item from a store's shelf, do you ever wonder how they got there? The answer is workers. People do jobs in our communities every day. They might be chefs, store clerks, or journalists. They may take care of animals, design clothing, or drive trucks. Many people receive money for doing their jobs. Others, such as moms and dads who stay at home to take care of their kids, or people who volunteer to help the elderly, might not be paid. But they are all doing different kinds of jobs.

Jobs are an important part of an economy. An economy is the production, distribution, and consumption of goods and services.

Firefighters have one of the most important jobs in a community. Volunteer firefighters serve their communities without getting paid.

compare and contrast

Some people start a job, discover their passion for it, and continue in the same field their whole lives as a career. Others may change to a different field with a new job. What is the difference between a job and a career?

Some people volunteer to take care of animals in a shelter, without expecting payment for their help. They do this because they care about animals, and because they want to do something special for their community.

Coworking

The products and services that people offer through their jobs are important for a community to function. Communities also need the exchange of money between buyers and sellers. People with jobs also buy homes and pay taxes. Taxes are fees paid to governments. They are used to provide many services, such as building schools and maintaining roads. People with jobs help their community, and even their country, function.

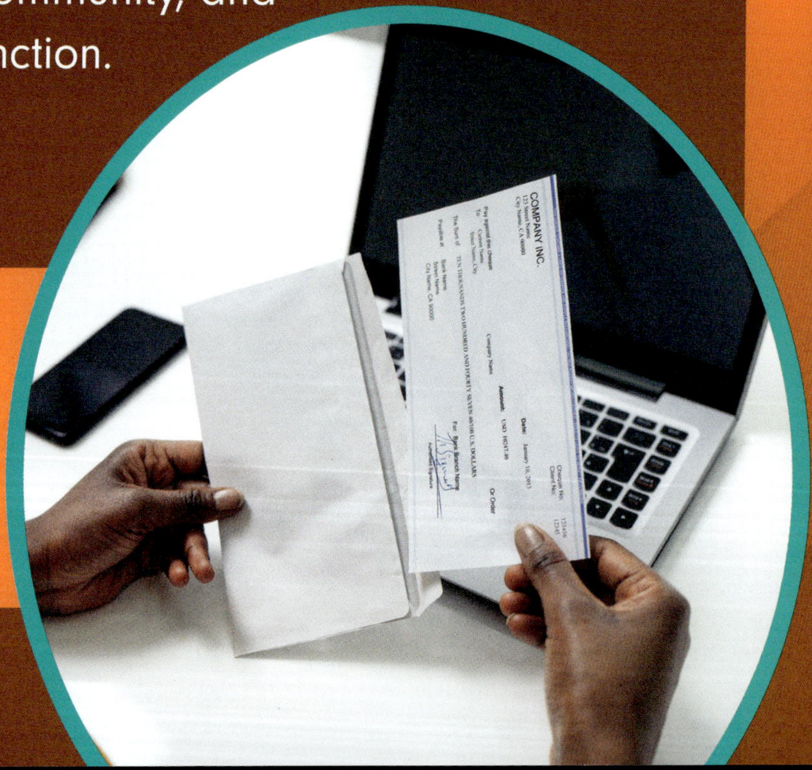

Members of a community need to have jobs so that they can make money to pay taxes and buy homes—helping the community function.

Public schools receive money from taxes so they can provide a good education for students.

Sometimes there's not enough jobs for everyone in a community. Stores close if people can't afford to buy things. Without a balance of buying and selling, the community cannot have a good economy. With fewer people paying taxes, there may be cutbacks on community helpers like police officers and firefighters. School **budgets** may also be cut. Some people may then find jobs in a new community or field.

WORD WISE

A BUDGET IS A PLAN FOR HOW MUCH MONEY WILL BE SPENT AND WHERE IT WILL BE SPENT. FAMILIES, BUSINESSES, AND GOVERNMENTS ALL USE BUDGETS TO GUIDE THEIR SPENDING.

The History of Work

Trading work in exchange for goods dates back centuries. This is called barter. For example, someone who had chopped a load of firewood might trade it for a pail of milk from a farmer. People performed jobs for each other in trade too. A blacksmith might shoe a horse in exchange for a carpenter repairing his front door.

Goods, such as animal skins and meat, used to be traded for services or other items people needed.

Labor unions are organized groups of workers in a particular job or field. They help to improve wages and working conditions for their fellow employees.

When people stopped being able to live on what they could grow and trade for, they began to take jobs to earn money. Many people began working in factories. They worked long hours for low pay. If they were sick or injured, they lost their jobs. Finally the government passed laws to improve working conditions. But some jobs still do not pay their workers enough money to buy the things they need.

Consider This

Do you think the barter system, as opposed to trading goods for money, would work today? Does money as payment seem like a better offer?

Defining "Job"

Not only do jobs help consumers who are receiving a service, but they allow workers to earn the money they need to live. This money might be actual cash, a paper check that they can cash at the bank, or an automatic deposit into their bank account. Employees also learn new skills. These skills might help them get other jobs later on. People also gain a feeling of self-respect and responsibility when they do a job well.

Paychecks can be deposited directly into a person's bank account, or they can be sent to the person as a check to be cashed at the bank.

Workers have to be trained for their job in order to know what to do. They are often trained by current employees, or even the employers themselves.

Employers pay employees to do work for them. In return for the money they pay people to do the jobs, employers get help making products and providing services. This helps their business stay healthy and even grow, ensuring that their employees will continue to have jobs.

Consider This

Some people, like firefighters or caregivers, volunteer their services and do not receive payment. Why do you think they do this?

Job Searching

People apply for jobs they're interested in, because they need money or want to pursue a particular field. Some people go to college or a **vocational school** to learn how to do certain jobs. Doctors and engineers go to school for many years to learn their jobs. Others find advertisements for jobs online or in newspapers and learn how to do the work on the job. Some people start their own business, such as a toy store, and work there.

Both colleges and vocational schools teach their students important skills for their fields.

Owning a business can be thrilling, but it requires a lot of hard work and responsibility.

A company may fire employees if they do their work poorly. Employees can be "laid off" or let go when a company can't afford to pay them. This can create a bad economic cycle. People without jobs cannot buy goods and services. This affects the businesses that make those goods and services because they will lose money and perhaps close.

WORD WISE

A VOCATIONAL SCHOOL TEACHES STUDENTS SKILLS FOR THEIR DESIRED OCCUPATIONS. THEY MIGHT LEARN TO BE DENTAL ASSISTANTS, PLUMBERS, OR ELECTRICIANS. THEY CAN ALSO LEARN SPECIAL SKILLS, SUCH AS HOW TO FIX MACHINES.

The Truth About Training

Depending on the job, years of training or a college degree may be required. A doctor may spend eight years in college and medical school plus many more years working in a hospital. A teacher usually goes to college for at least four years. A police officer must undergo training at an academy. They learn special skills and have to be physically fit. Many people keep learning even after they have jobs.

Because they need so much training, these kinds of jobs often pay more than other jobs. The people who do them are very important to the community because they have these special skills and knowledge. The economy is able to flourish because of the services provided.

Doctors may spend more than 15 years in college and medical school before they can treat people.

compare and contrast

Certain careers, such as doctors or surgeons, pay more than others, such as teachers or police officers. Why do you think this is? Are some jobs considered more important than other jobs?

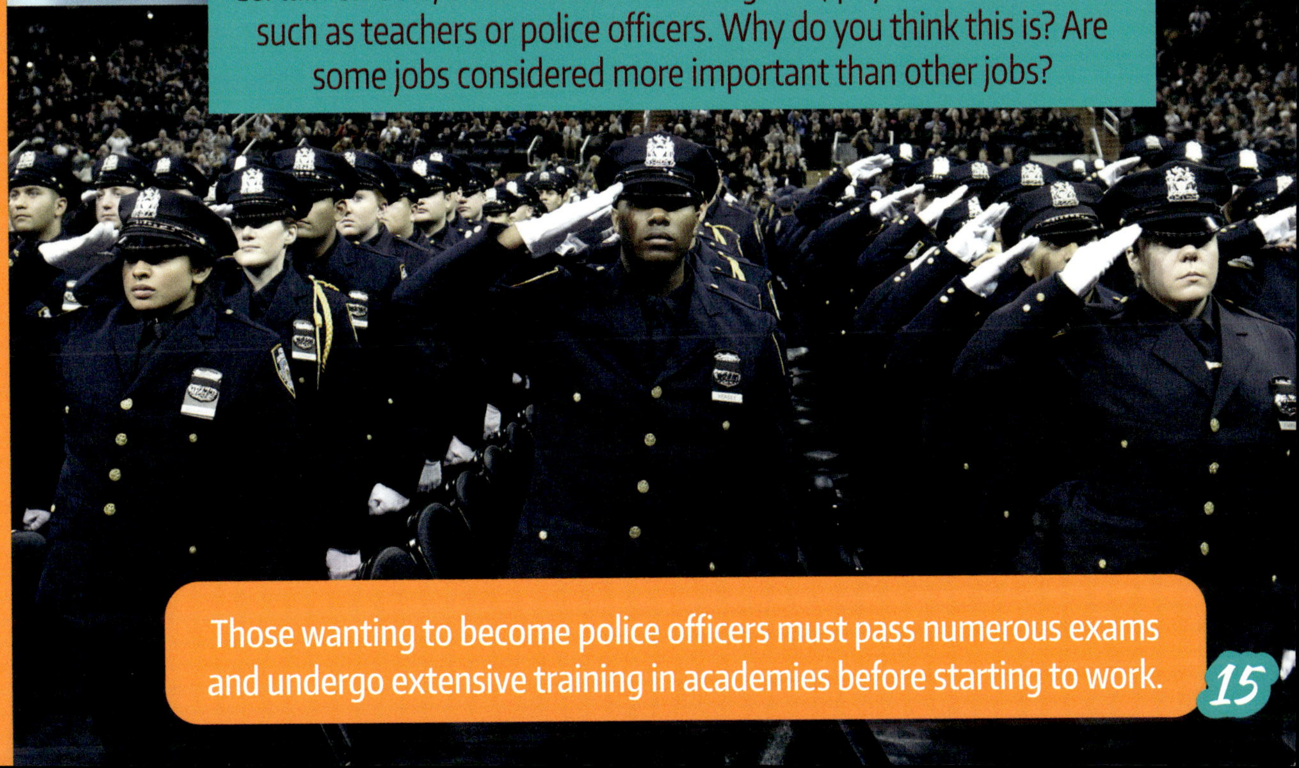

Those wanting to become police officers must pass numerous exams and undergo extensive training in academies before starting to work.

Making It from Scratch

Many workers in a community are trained to create products. They are sometimes called producers. Producers include craftsmen like carpenters and builders. They also include people who make clothing or work in a factory that makes cars or computers. Electricians and plumbers, who can help build new homes and other buildings or repair old ones, are also producers.

Craftspeople may serve as apprentices before working on their own. That means they work alongside someone who is already a master in that field to learn the trade.

Bread is made with wheat and sugar—two things that bakers must acquire from farmers.

Farmers produce food for people and animals to eat. They raise animals. They might also produce wool or cotton for clothes or trees for building. There are also producers who bake bread or make cheese, using the goods from farmers and turning them into products that community members need.

Consider This

Hundreds of years ago, it was normal for most people to grow their own food or make their own clothing at home. Nowadays, we mainly pay other people to do this for us. What do you think changed?

Customer Service

Those who provide customers with a service are another important type of worker. Most people cannot fix their own plumbing or cut their own hair. They need other people to do these jobs for them. In a restaurant, cooks and servers are needed to make and bring customers their food. If someone needs a coat mended, they go to a tailor.

People who own stores provide a service by selling certain things such as food or clothes or hardware. Nurses, bank tellers, and flight attendants also provide services.

compare and contrast

In the United States, it's common for people to tip certain workers who offer services, such as waiters and hairstylists. However, most professionals, such as lawyers and doctors, are not tipped for their services. Why might this be the case?

Hairstylists and pet groomers provide services that most people couldn't do on their own.

Car dealerships offer the opportunity for people to purchase or lease cars. They also sell spare car parts and offer maintenance services.

An Artistic Eye

Many people are gifted with talents in art, music, or writing—they're considered to have an artistic eye! They search for jobs that use their talents. They may play the piano, sing, conduct symphony orchestras, or play drums in a rock band. Other people lead church choirs or play church organs. Some paint beautiful paintings or create sculptures. Some other people act on stage or in movies. Or perhaps they write books, poetry, or magazine articles.

Jobs like these contribute different kinds of arts to the community. They provide something beyond the basic needs of everyday life. Some people who work in the arts make a great deal of money. Others do it solely because it is their passion, even if they're not paid much.

compare and contrast

Famous actors and musicians are paid millions of dollars to create art, while actors and musicians who perform locally in their own communities don't make as much. Why do you think some artists make more money than others?

A talented musician can make money by performing a concert for fans and writing music that plays on the radio or streaming services.

Photographers might work for a company, or they might freelance. Freelance refers to an artist who works for themselves or submits their work to different companies at the same time.

Community and Country

Certain jobs involve workers serving their community or country—or both. However, these jobs might require them to live outside of their community. People who **enlist** in the military may live far from home. They may even fight in wars and risk their lives to protect their homes, their states, and their country.

Men and women who enlist in the Marine Corps may spend years on, above, or below the water—far from home.

Local, state, and federal are the three different levels of government employees.

Many people work at government jobs. They may work in their town or city government. They may be elected to serve at the state level. Some are elected to serve in Washington, D.C., representing their state in the federal government. Some examples of government jobs are those who work for the postal service and national parks.

WORD WISE

A PERSON WHO WANTS TO JOIN THE MILITARY MUST ENLIST. TO ENLIST MEANS THEY AGREE TO SERVE FOR A SET AMOUNT OF TIME.

Decision-Making

Some people have careers that span decades. It may be because they love it, or because they spent years in school or training to learn it. Others have many jobs. This might be because they like trying new things. Sometimes the company or business they work for no longer needs them. Some companies go out of business, and their employees lose their jobs.

If a person really connects with their work, they may stay at the same company or in the same field for many years—even until they retire.

Oftentimes interns are students. Internships help students decide what field they want to pursue after graduation.

If people are interested in their work, they are more likely to keep their job. It's important for people to think about whether they would like a job before they start it. They might do an **internship** to try out a job. There are also tests that people take to show them what kinds of jobs would fit them best. People who join the police academy or military often take these tests.

WORD WISE

AN INTERNSHIP IS WHEN A PERSON HOLDS A TEMPORARY POSITION IN A COMPANY. THEY CAN LEARN A SET OF SKILLS AND DECIDE WHETHER THEY LIKE THE FIELD. SOME INTERNS ARE PAID, BUT OTHERS ARE NOT.

Trying Something New

When a new business opens, they're probably going to need to hire workers to help them. It might hire people who already have experience in that business or people who need training. Communities like to have new businesses open and hire people. It helps the economy by creating new jobs. It also attracts people to live there.

Some businesses are locally owned, while others are franchised. A franchise is when a company allows individual businesses to sell the rights to their products or services for payment. This is common with popular restaurant chains, such as Subway and McDonalds.

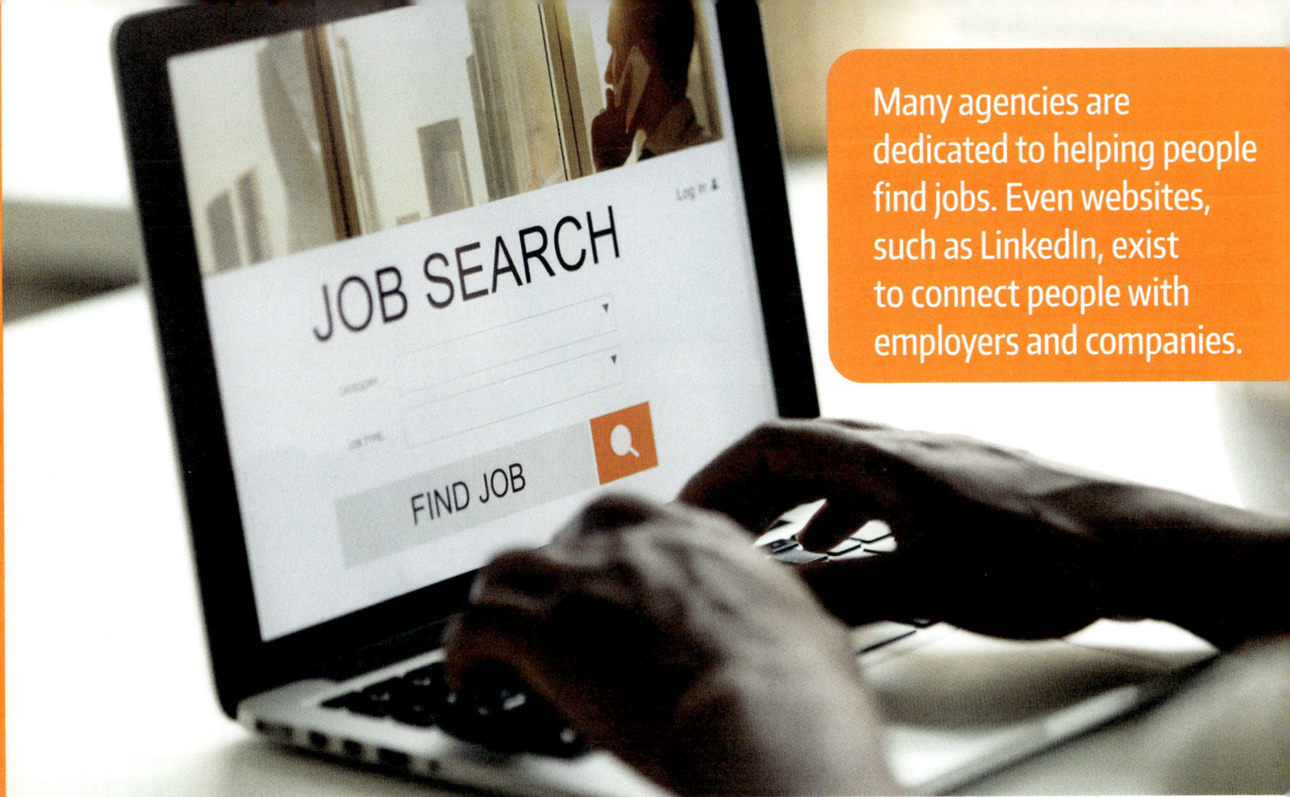

Many agencies are dedicated to helping people find jobs. Even websites, such as LinkedIn, exist to connect people with employers and companies.

When people lose jobs they can get help from their community or state. They can receive unemployment payments. This is money from the government to help them pay their bills until they find a new job. There are also community organizations that help people find jobs, get training, and receive education.

Consider This

Unemployment services created to help those without a job did not always exist in America. How do unemployment benefits help those without a job? How do unemployment benefits help the community?

Helping Hands

Earning money is necessary in our modern society for people to support their lifestyles. They need jobs and the earnings they create to support themselves as well as their families. Communities cannot survive without people doing jobs. These jobs provide services people in the community need and want. Jobs also provide products that people in the community buy. Jobs help bring tax dollars to the community as well.

Jobs and earnings work together. A healthy economy is made possible through the hard work people contribute to the communities they live within.

compare and contrast

Some workers, such as carpenters and electricians, are paid by the hour. Others, such as veterinarians, receive a salary. This means they receive an annual sum on a monthly or yearly basis. What do you think decides the way a job pays its employees? Is one way better than the other?

People can earn money by working all sorts of jobs. They can be employed by the government, a private business, or their own companies.

Members of a community help it to thrive by working together and creating a healthy economy.

Glossary

account A sum of money deposited in a bank.

advertisement A public notice or announcement, such as for a job vacancy.

afford To be able to pay for something.

agency A part of a government that manages projects in a certain area.

blacksmith A worker who shapes iron (as into horseshoes) by heating it and then hammering it into shape on an iron block.

civilization A large group of people who share certain advanced ways of living and working.

conditions The circumstances affecting the way people live or work.

deposit Money placed in a bank to keep it safe.

elderly Relating to later life or older persons.

elected To select someone by vote for an office, position, or membership.

electrician A person who installs, operates, or repairs electrical equipment.

employee One who works for another for wages or a salary.

engineer A person who designs, builds, or maintains engines, machines, or public works.

fired When someone is dismissed from their job.

function To serve a certain purpose, or to work.

orchestra An assembly of musicians that performs musical works written for a group.

plumber A person who puts in or repairs the pipes and fixtures involved in the distribution and use of water in a building.

unemployment The state of not having a job.

volunteer Someone who offers to do something without being paid.

For More Information

Books

Flynn, Sarah Wassner. *Not-So-Common Cents: Super Duper Important Facts About Money You Can't Afford to Miss.* Washington, D.C.: National Geographic Kids, 2023.

Kishtainy, Niall. *The Economics Book: Big Ideas Simply Explained.* New York, NY: DK, 2018.

Lee, Kelly. *What Is Supply and Demand? Little Economists.* San Jose, CA: Econ for Kids, 2022.

Websites

Economics
jr.brainpop.com/socialstudies/economics/
Learn more about goods and services and needs and wants through informative videos and fun games.

Money and Finance, Supply and Demand
www.ducksters.com/money/economics.php
Money and the economy are explored on this detailed website.

Publisher's note to educators and parents: Our editors have carefully reviewed these websites to ensure that they are suitable for students. Many websites change frequently, however, and we cannot guarantee that a site's future contents will continue to meet our high standards of quality and educational value. Be advised that students should be closely supervised whenever they access the internet.

Index